I Mo
You
Cheese

"If this book had been available twenty years ago, I would have caught the bus from Pietermaritzburg to Durban. Which is to say: this book will not help you in the long run."

– Bruce Fordyce, multiple winner of the Comrades ultra-marathon

"I imagine myself laminating this book, so that it doesn't become dog-eared, and reading it on winter's nights to my grandchildren beside an open fire, and telling them: this is what will happen to you if you don't finish your law degree."

– James Weil, senior partner: Fly, Weil, Weil, Weil, Schuster and Weil

"Reading this book made no appreciable difference to my life."

– John Robbie, former international rugby player,
current radio and television personality

"When I finished reading *I Moved Your Cheese*, I thought about my own life and I realised: Things aren't so bad after all."

– anonymous testimonial, Fancourt Golf Estate

"No Amazonian rainforests were harmed in the making of this book."

– Sting

"Darrel Bristow-Bovey is a very persistent writer."

– Clare O'Donoghue, editor, *Style* magazine

"Darrel Bristow-Bovey writes in the stirring and time-honoured tradition of Louis L'Amour and Kilroy."

– Jeremy Gordin, managing editor, *Sunday Independent* newspaper

"No!"

– Mike Lipkin, motivational speaker

"I always knew Darrel would write a book, but I could never have guessed it would be about cheese. He never seemed to be that interested in cheese when he was younger. He liked macaroni-and-cheese, of course – what growing boy doesn't? – but if someone had said to me twenty years ago: 'Roslyn, what will your son write his first book about?' I would not have said cheese. I don't know what I would have said, but not cheese. Ice cream, maybe. He liked ice cream."

– Roslyn Bristow-Bovey, the author's mother

"I know I still owe Darrel a beer, but I will not say what you want me to say."

– Jeremy Maggs, South African presenter, *Who Wants to Be a Millionaire?*

"I think there is something wrong with Darrel Bristow-Bovey."

– Tim Modise, SAfm talk-show host

"I have not read this book."

– Felicia Mabuza-Suttle, talk-show host

"There is a cold front over Gordonia."

– Graeme Hart, weatherman

"I found this book so moving that I bought a copy for everyone in my workplace, and I intend giving out copies as Christmas presents to everyone I meet."

– Marlene Fryer, publisher

"I have on many occasions considered changing my life, but thanks to Darrel I will stay just the way I am till the day I die."

– Bill, retired

"Not a word in this book is true."

– Chunko

FORTHCOMING TITLES BY THE SAME AUTHOR

Cheese Got a Ticket to Ride

Please Cheese Me

Cheese Guevara: The Motorcycle Diaries

East of Edam

The Unbearable Lightness of Brie

The Madness of King Gorgonzola

In the Camembert of Strangers

More Haste, Less Cheese

Songs from Cheese Aznavour

Rumplestilton

The Emmental Strikes Back

Return of the Cheddar

Cheeses Died For Our Sins

To Brie or Not to Brie

How Now Brown Gouda

We'll Always Have Parmesan

Sex, Drugs and Roquefort

Home, Cheese, and Don't Spare the Horses

You Can Lead a Gouda Water, But You Can't Make It Float

I Moved Your Cheese

DARREL BRISTOW-BOVEY

Published in the UK in 2002
by New Holland Publishers (UK) Ltd

First published 2001

3 5 7 9 10 8 6 4 2

Publishing Manager: Marlene Fryer
Managing Editor: Robert Plummer
Editor: Martha Evans
Cover and Text Designer: Natascha Adendorff
Typesetter: Monique van den Berg

Reproduction by Hirt & Carter Cape (Pty) Ltd
Printed and bound by Athenæum Press Ltd

ISBN 1 84330 165 2

www.newhollandpublishers.com

Contents

This book is dedicated to all those who made the writing of it possible:

Jack Daniel; Leon the barman; whoever taught Braam van Straaten how to kick; Peter Stuyvesant; Marco Polo (for inventing the pizza, or bringing it back from China, or something of the sort, I forget now). And of course Justine, the little cheese.

Introduction

This is not another self-help book. It really isn't. I wouldn't do that to you. Self-help books are damaging to the self-esteem. Self-help books are like diets, or the gym contract some bastard relative gave you for your birthday: they promise to help you, but really they mock you. They build up your expectations, and then they leave you feeling low and craven and flinching at loud noises and sudden movements.

Self-help books are damaging to the self-esteem. They promise to help you, but really they mock you.

Like diets and gym contracts, self-help books offer the illusion that you can do something to significantly improve yourself – you can become slimmer, wiser, more attractive to air hostesses or that guy who works in the accounts department and rides a motorbike on weekends. You will draw upon yourself good fortune and the golden blessings of a universe that looks on you and is well pleased with what it sees. Self-help books lift you aloft on the wings of hope and then, when you have failed once more, they drop you like a losing lottery ticket, face-down like a piece of buttered toast.

Self-help books, to be brief, are no good, and the reason is plain: they expect you to do all the work. Taken to its logical conclusion, a self-help book would be a collection of blank pages and a pen. (A proposal, incidentally, which sadly found scant favour with my publisher when first I pitched it. I even brought my own sheaf of foolscap and a ballpoint pen which I stole when signing the security register in the downstairs lobby. "Look," I said persuasively, "I can already give you the manuscript." Publishers, alas, are made of sterner stuff.)

No matter how quick and easy they promise to be, self-help books have the common failing of requiring you to put in some effort. *The Seven Spiritual Laws of Success*, say, may seem to have achieved the astonishing feat of condensing several millennia of accumulated cultural learning into seven convenient bite-sized chunks, like so many KFC nuggets of deep-fried wisdom, but you are still expected to memorise the laws, or at least scribble them down on the back of your hand, and then, I suppose, do something about them. This is the fundamental truth that writers of self-help books overlook: if we were capable or even likely to do these things for ourselves, we wouldn't need their poxy books.

If you are like me – and deep down I think you are – you aren't mad keen on working hard to improve yourself. Human beings are a little like Liberia or the Durban beach-front or London's Millennium Dome: there is not really a lot you can do to make them fundamentally better. By the time you realise there's a problem, there's not much else for it but to tear it all down and start over again. Speaking for myself – and I hasten to point out that I am neither the Durban beachfront nor Liberia, although on occasion certain so-called friends have pointed out an alleged physical similarity to the Millennium Dome – that all seems like a little too much trouble.

I am here to tell you that that is okay. Don't be ashamed; say it with me: We are lazy, we are idle, we are downright inert, and we don't give a damn. We are the secret truth of society, the bedrock upon which any decent civilisation is built. We are the yawning majority who can't quite believe that firming up our bellies and becoming nicer human beings really will be worth the kind of effort demanded of us. We have always been here, and we will be here a long time after the fanatical self-improvers have shuffled off to their just rewards.

Say it with me: We are lazy, we are idle, we are downright inert, and we don't give a damn.

What's more, we have nothing of which to be ashamed. We are the best part of this tawdry world. You don't see us invading neighbouring countries or launching political parties. None of us invented boy bands or cellphones that ring with the theme tune from *The Good, the Bad and the Ugly*. We couldn't be bothered. We just want the quiet life. We want to eat well, live well, have sex with attractive people, perhaps drive a fast car on the open road while drinking a beer, but we are not prepared to bend the laws of nature to do it. We prefer to slipstream in evolution's wake.

If it weren't for us, this world would be a bleaker place. We are, for instance, solely responsible for almost every item of dinner-party conversation worth hearing. The snappy aphorism, the casual item of waspish gossip, the – if you will pardon the expression – *bon mot* were all invented by people like us: people interested in maximum effect for minimum effort. If it weren't for us, it would be all personal trainers and striving toward the light and embracing change and similar appalling notions. We are interested in none of that. If it weren't for us, this world would implode from boredom.

Of course, this is no reason to get complacent. Like the stegosaurus or the fondue set with matching forks (which, let no one tell you different, is not cool and never will be again), if we fail to adapt to the changing times, we are doomed to extinction. We will be banished to the back of the kitchen cupboard; Steven Spielberg will make movies about us. We need to learn to stay attractive to our mates, to stay wealthy and healthy and secretly to thrive, that we might pass our genes to the generations that follow slouching in our shadow.

Like the stegosaurus or the fondue set with matching forks, if we fail to adapt to the changing times, we are doomed to extinction.

That is why I have written this book. If you want to take three easy steps to being a fabulous person with a wonderful life, close this book immediately. This is not the book for you (although you should feel free to buy several copies for your friends). This is the self-help book for people who want to take no steps at all. This is the self-help book for people lying on the sofa. This book will tell you how to reap the rewards of being a better person, without having to trouble yourself with the unnecessary burden of actually becoming better.

(It is not even necessary to read this book. Simply buying it and keeping it displayed in a prominent position will make you brighter, happier and more desirable. Our pages have been treated with a revolutionary new formula that allows wisdom, through a process we have patented under the name Osmatix™, to pass directly from the page into the atmosphere, where it can easily be inhaled from a reclining position. In countries of the northern hemisphere where this book is on sale, you can identify Osmatix™ by its mild aroma of cooking oil. In the southern hemisphere it is characterised by the slight odour of stilton.

If you would like to take advantage of this unique opportunity, we have provided a number of blank pages at the back of this book. Besides making the book look thicker on the shelves, these pages will allow you to pretend to be reading – at the beach, perhaps, or on public transport – while in fact giving you the opportunity to rest your eyes and think about last night's episode of *Sex and the City*.

Alas, however, if you are planning to share this book with your life-partner or members of your immediate family or your colleagues at work, it is my duty to inform you that Osmatix™ is a highly sophisticated compound. Like a gosling newly hatched, it bonds and imprints itself to the particular chemical properties of whoever first opens this book and breathes its heady scent. The Osmatix™ of this book will work for you, and you alone. Your husband or your secretary will just have to buy their own copy. This obviously is bad news for you, but good news for us. In fact, to members of the publishing industry, the smell of Osmatix™ resembles nothing so much as newly folded money.)

So follow me, brothers and sisters, into a brave – well, bravish – new world. A world, at any rate, in which our cowardice is well hidden. And as we go, remember our mantra. Whisper it to yourself. Print it on a card and keep it prominently displayed on your refrigerator door or the dashboard of your car. Have it tattooed inside your eyelids, so that you can read it while you take your afternoon nap. If you like, you can strip to the waist, take out your drums and chant the mantra to the steady pulse-beat of your throbbing bongos. (Although if you do choose to go the half-naked drumming route, I must ask you to go down to the bottom of the garden and crouch in the shrubbery where decent folk can't see you.)

Do you have the mantra ready? Do you? Oh. Sorry, I thought I had told you already. Our mantra is: "Anything can be faked." You can add any ohms and ahs and ululations you might require, but that is the gist of it: anything can be faked.

Our mantra is: "Anything can be faked."

(Except insincerity, I suppose. It is difficult to fake insincerity. And having bad hair; that is something that can't be faked. You either have bad hair or you don't, I'm afraid. But other than these things, the mantra holds pretty much true.)

Are we ready now? Are we? Right, follow me.

1
Seeking and Finding

It is not easy being a lazy person in today's world. Mind you, this is in fact true of almost every age. The bustling mob has no appreciation of the effort it takes to be idle. It demands patience and application and a stubborn refusal to listen to reason. Only we will ever know what discipline and dedication is required to further our art. It is our burden to bear alone, alas, alas.

The bustling mob has no appreciation of the effort it takes to be idle. It demands patience and application and a stubborn refusal to listen to reason.

Still, today we are assailed ever more ruthlessly with the injunction to make ourselves better – to look better, to tell the truth more often, to drink less, to be one with the angels.

Once when I was younger and more active, I too turned to the world to seek the secret of a more perfect life. I travelled to South America, to Chile and the hot wastes of the Atacama desert, where I heard tell of a wise man who lived in the mountains. I couldn't miss him, the locals said, pointing to a narrow footpath that led up between the bleached-white rocks into the o'er-looming crags. He was old and bearded and would probably appear on top of a rock and pelt me with mangoes when I got to the really steep part.

"Where does he find mangoes in the middle of the desert?" I asked. The locals lowered their gaze and drew patterns in the sand with their toes.

"The old man of the mountains works in mysterious ways," they said.

So I packed a knapsack and a waterproof jacket and headed for the hills. It was hot and dry, but that is what you expect of a desert. When I reached the really steep part, I pulled the waterproof jacket over my head. No one likes to be pelted with mangoes. But as I climbed higher and higher up the really steep part, I couldn't help noticing that the old man of the mountains had not appeared. How was I to find the old man of the mountains, if he wasn't going to attack me with sun-ripened tropical fruit? And this was the first piece of wisdom the old man of the mountains taught me:

> *I was expecting the worst, but now that the worst has not arrived, I am disappointed. I am the architect of my own dismay.*

Actually, that was the second piece of wisdom. The first was:

> *If you are climbing the really steep part of a mountain with a waterproof jacket over your head, you cannot see*

where you are going and consequently it should come as no surprise if you bark your shin on a rock.

So I removed my waterproof jacket from my head, and as I stood rubbing my shin I saw that before me was a rocky ledge, and sitting there, legs crossed and eyes closed, was a ragged old man with a long ragged beard. I gasped and dropped to his feet, partly from reverence, partly because it had been a long climb in the thin air and none of the locals had wanted to sell me any coca leaves. When the dry heaves stopped, I thought of this important life lesson:

If we are not afraid of tropical fruits falling on our heads, we will be better able to see the riches in front of us.

I wrote it in the sand with my finger, in case I forgot it later.

I wasn't sure how to approach the old man of the mountains. His eyes were still closed and his breathing was deep and regular, as is common with mountain sages and also didgeridoo players. I reached out a trembling hand and tugged at the hem of his loincloth.

The old man of the mountains gave a little start and a snuffle and opened his eyes. They were molten and golden, like brimming cups of bourbon. He raised his eyes unto the sky and uttered these words: "What the hell?"

"I am your humble pilgrim," I said, rubbing my hair against his feet.

"How did you get up the really steep part without me hearing you?" demanded the old man of the mountains, kicking me in the head.

I was startled, but not shocked. Ragged old sages can be notoriously prickly. My good friend Chunko once visited a sage in the steaming jungles of Laos who lost his temper after a game of backgammon and beat Chunko about the head and shoulders with a length of bamboo, and also with a brick. "Sometimes," says Chunko sadly, "sages have to teach you the hard way."

Meanwhile, I was scrawling another life lesson in the dust with my forefinger:

> *Do not be afraid of discovering that your idols have feet of clay. If they have clay feet, it won't hurt so much when they kick you in the head.*

Happily, the old man of the mountains soon stopped kicking me in the head. He settled back to catch some more shut-eye. "Master," I implored, "I am your servant."

"If you're my servant," he said, adjusting his loincloth, "go keep an eye open for any more pilgrims coming up the path. I have a week's supply of mangoes, and I don't want them to spoil."

"But Master," I said, "I am here to learn from you." He tried to kick me in the head again, but I seized his leg and twisted it and wrestled him to the ground. It was an awkward situation, of course, but there was nothing for it but to keep going, pausing only to write this life lesson in the sand:

> *Wisdom does not drop from the sky like mangoes. Sometimes you need to wrestle with wisdom and put it*

in a half-nelson. Do not be afraid of wrestling with wisdom: if it has been sitting cross-legged on a mountaintop for any considerable length of time, it will probably be slightly malnourished and easily manhandled.

"Okay, okay," said the old man of the mountains in a muffled voice, "if you let me up I'll answer your questions."

So we sat facing each other, and an air of great calm settled between us.

Do not be afraid of wrestling with wisdom: if it has been sitting cross-legged on a mountaintop for any considerable length of time, it will probably be slightly malnourished and easily manhandled.

"How," I asked, "does one become a wise old man of the mountains?"

He shrugged and sniffed and swished his beard in the air. "Not much to it," he said, and told this story:

"I was a young man, much like yourself, seeking enlightenment. I met a man who claimed to be Carlos Castaneda, although looking back, I realise it might have been Carlos Santana. Everybody said he was a very wise man and played a nifty guitar, and he gave me a piece of cactus to chew on. At the time I thought: 'If this man is so wise, why doesn't he remove the thorns from the cactus before chewing it?', but I was young then, and easily swayed by the offer of hallucinogenic drugs.

"So I ate the cactus and a number of extraordinary things happened. I was vouchsafed a vision of the inner workings of life and eternity. I scribbled it down in the sand with my forefinger, because I knew I would forget later, but you know how it goes with scribbling things in the sand. It's all very well, but you can't take it with you.

"And then, once the vision of the inner workings of life and eternity had passed, it was replaced by a sharp-toothed demon visiting me in the guise of Snoopy."

I had to interrupt. "Snoopy?" I said.

"Yes, Snoopy. He's not as innocent as he looks, that dog. Snoopy chased me, and I fled. I fled from Central America. I fled with that hound of hell at my heels, until finally I fetched up here. By that time, I don't know, I guess the cactus had worn off. Snoopy had vanished. But I was pretty tired, as you can imagine, so I decided to rest up a spell. Rental is not as cheap as you would imagine in Chile, so I found this rocky ledge and here I am. It's comfortable enough, except when it rains and when rattlesnakes come looking for warmth and try to curl up in my armpits on chilly nights."

"Does it rain much?" I asked.

"Not for the last twenty years," he said, with the smug look of a man who has invested wisely in real estate.

"But what about being a sage?" I persisted.

"Oh, that," he shrugged. "I had been up here a while, eating the eggs from a condor nest and wondering what I should do next. I was thinking of going down to Patagonia to write a travel book, or maybe New York to try my hand at musical comedy, when I heard a commotion from below. Three locals came clambering up carrying a basket of foodstuffs, including a big wheel of llama cheese. I do love llama cheese."

"Really?" I said. "I find it too tangy."

"Not at all, kid. You need to learn to appreciate cheese. Anyway, they gave me that food in return for any words of wisdom I might have. I told them I didn't really have any, and offered to recite the first two verses of 'Puff the Magic Dragon' instead. They nodded and bowed, so I did. Then they went away, nudging each other with their elbows. And then I realised they didn't speak English. But it didn't seem to matter. Each day different villagers came to visit, carrying a basket of foodstuffs, and they would sit and listen to 'Puff the Magic Dragon', or sometimes, if I was in the mood, the Beatles' 'Ob-la-di Ob-la-da'."

I nodded at his tale, and as I nodded I wrote this life lesson in the sand:

> *Sometimes it is not necessary to learn wisdom by being taught wisdom. Sometimes it is enough merely to be in the proximity of wisdom. Sometimes wisdom doesn't even have to make sense.*

But to tell you the truth, I was getting a little tired of writing down these life lessons. And I was beginning to doubt the wisdom of listening much longer to the wise old man of the mountains. I was ready to go. "One last thing," I said. "Why the mangoes?"

The old man of the mountains tapped his nose and winked. "Everybody has to have a gimmick," he said. "There's a travelling salesman who makes deliveries once a week. He comes up the back way, so the locals can't see him. There's actually a road back there – he just drives on up in his Peugeot. He's trying to persuade me to switch to papaya. They are more expensive, but they are squishier; plus he can supply me with canned papaya, which keeps for longer."

The old man of the mountains tapped his nose and winked. "Everybody has to have a gimmick," he said.

I nodded and slowly set off down the long path to the world below. I had a bad feeling that I knew what was going to happen next. I was right. He had a good arm for a raggedy old man – he had beaned me with four papayas and what felt like a yam before I was even halfway down the really steep part. I couldn't really blame him, I suppose – no one likes being put in a half-nelson – but I do wish he had taken the papayas out of their cans first.

FOOTNOTE

How I wish that were the end of the story. Sadly it is not. I roamed the world for some years, seeking wisdom in a more and more desultory fashion, until one day, swaying in a hammock on a squid fishing boat being lashed by a monsoon in the South China Sea, I thought to myself: "Sod it. I'm going home. It's warm there, and I can watch television."

So I bought my ticket. But as I stood in the airport bookshop, waiting for my flight to be called, my eye happened to alight on the best-seller rack. And on the rack was a book, and on the cover of the book was the photograph of a man's face. *Hang about!* I thought. *I know that face!*

And I did know that face, although the last time I had seen it, it had been rather more grimy and streaked with dirt from being on the wrong end of a half-nelson. The book was titled *Go Tell It on the Mountain*, and on the cover it had a little red sticker in the shape of a star, with the words "Over one million copies sold" written in white letters.

The book was subtitled: *Ten lessons learnt from a life more perfect.* I could scarcely bring myself to open it, but I did. The first chapter began with these words:

"If we are not afraid of tropical fruits falling on our heads, we will be better able to see the riches in front of us."

I closed the book and caught my flight, and I memorised this final life lesson, which I shall never write in the sand, and which I shall never forget:

If you have no wisdom of your own, reading self-help books will not help you. You will have to write them instead.

2
Finding Your Egg

Gurus on mountain tops, you will have gathered, are no good for our purposes. They are no good for anyone's purposes, come to that, but for the lazy person they are worse than useless. Even if he is actually a guru, rather than a nut without a razor living rent-free in the wilderness, it is so much trouble trying to find him that by the time you get there all you want is a beer and a taxi back home again. Fortunately, I have a story close to hand that tells us all we need to know.

Listen now to this tale. It is a simple tale, but one, I think we can agree, that speaks to our innermost hearts. What's more, it incorporates ancient folklore and the wisdom of a vanishing culture, which I understand is very fashionable nowadays.

It is a story from the indigenous peoples of southern Africa. You might call them the Bushmen, or you might call them the San, or you might call them by the name they use, although if you do that, neither of us will be able to spell or pronounce it, so we won't really know what we're talking about. Whatever their name nowadays, they are the oldest people of a very old continent, and they know a thing or two.

I was told this tale by a very wizened fellow wearing a cloak of antelope hide who sat next to me on a Greyhound bus. He wore nothing else besides his antelope-hide cloak, which made for awkward moments and a reluctance on my part to squeeze past him to go to the bathroom. Besides a severely distended bladder, the wizened old fellow gave me this gift of wisdom – a gift I have shared with many others over the years. They found it helpful, and I think you will too.

This tale incorporates ancient folklore and the wisdom of a vanishing culture, which is very fashionable nowadays.

THE STORY OF THE EGG

Many moons, and moons of moons, ago, when the animals still covered the land and humans roamed free, there was a young man named Xam. That was really his name – Xam.

Xam was young but he was a good hunter. He could track an ostrich across a gravel plain with his loincloth tied over his eyes, which always impressed the girls, and he was a dab hand with a blow-dart. At night he would lie awake and purse his lips and make short, sharp exhalations of breath. When his mother said: "What are you doing over there?" he would reply: "I am practising my blow-darting technique."

And she would say: "Well, just you keep your hands above the animal-hide blanket, where I can see them."

Xam dreamed of hunting the desert elephant, for he believed that only when a young hunter had tracked and killed the mighty desert elephant would he truly be a man.

Does this sound familiar to you? Have you lain awake and dreamt of hunting the desert elephant? Do you still lie awake and purse your lips and make short, sharp exhalations of breath? Of course, your desert elephant might not have been an actual desert elephant. A desert elephant, we can safely say without ruining the ending, is a metaphor. Perhaps you lived nowhere near the desert. Perhaps your elephant was a luxury German sedan. Perhaps it was success, fame and the admiration of your peers. Perhaps it was Mrs Dunstable, your form five History teacher. There are as many desert elephants as there are types of cheese. More, probably.

One day some of the older boys came to Xam and said: "We are leaving to track the desert elephant. We will be away for many days and nights. We want you to come with us. You are a dab hand with a blow-dart; plus you never know when we might meet a gravel plain and an ostrich, although if you don't mind we'd rather you leave your loincloth where it is."

And Xam was overjoyed, and he went to ask permission of his mother. And his mother said: "No."

So Xam said: "All right, in that case can I spend the night with my friend Xab in his family's cave?"

And his mother said: "All right, but if you only return in a month's time, dragging a desert elephant behind you, you are going to be in big trouble, my boy."

But of course Xam joined the older boys and they set off on their journey to track the mighty desert elephant. They travelled light, as people did in those days, and as we would too if we didn't have pockets, but they did carry ostrich eggs that had been emptied out and filled with water and bunged up again with small sticks and wadded bits of animal hide. Animal hide was big with Xam's tribe. We use plastic – they used animal hide. Along the way, across the wide sandy wastes, they would each bury their ostrich eggs, one a day, and leave small markers in the sand.

Is this like your life? Do you leave behind important items, perhaps even important people, in the expectation that one day you will meet up with them again? Do you? Really? What sort of markers do you use? I have been thinking about it, and I can't quite figure out how the markers fit in with that analogy. But I couldn't leave them out, because, as we shall see, the markers are an important part of the story.

Because he had left home in a hurry, Xam had brought only one ostrich eggshell – a great big one, which he buried beneath a baobab tree.

The boys were away a long time, treading the hot sands of the African desert, and they only stopped when they reached the sea, and even then they had waded in a little way before someone suggested it was time to turn back.

One day, on the way back, they saw the tracks of the mighty desert elephant, and they set off in pursuit. They walked and walked, following the tracks. A few days later, one of the older boys cleared his throat and tapped Xam on the shoulder. "Are you sure we're walking the right way?" he said. They all stopped and looked at each other.

"What do you mean?" said Xam, a little defensively.

"I mean," said the older boy, "are we sure we know which side of a desert elephant's footprint is the front bit, and which part is the back bit?"

They all looked at each other again, then they all looked at Xam. Xam looked at the footprint. "Well ..." he said slowly, but then he stopped, because he didn't really know what else to say.

"Have you ever seen the track of the desert elephant before?" demanded the older boys.

Xam, who had kind of assumed that someone else had been leading the way, looked slowly down at the sand again, and said, "Weeellll ..."

There followed an ugly scene, involving some scrapping and kicking and biting and – though I am sorry to say so – swearing. At the end of it, they began the long walk back home. "We could always follow the wild elephant tracks back the other way," someone suggested under his breath, but everyone was glad he didn't repeat it.

Has this ever happened to you? Have you followed your desert elephant into the wilds, only to discover that when you stop to think about it, you don't know whether you are coming or going? Yes? Then did your friends beat you up? No? Good. You have chosen your friends wisely.

So they walked into the great, wide, brown desert. They crossed a gravel plain, and Xam could swear that he could make out the three-toed print of a desert ostrich. He looked up and was about to say something, but he noticed the older boys were all watching him with dark looks on their faces, so he closed his mouth again.

Every so often one of the older boys would recognise a small heap of stones or a twisted piece of wood, and scramble over the sand to dig up the egg that he had buried. Each time he would glug back the water himself, or share it with a friend. No one ever shared his water with Xam. Xam lived off the moisture he squeezed from small lizards and scorpions, which was fine, but not the same as a cooling eggshell of water. Besides, it is no fun, squeezing the moisture from a scorpion. They don't wriggle as much as the lizards, but they have very bad tempers. Xam thought about his mother waiting for him back at the cave, and he began to wish he hadn't come.

Then, as they reached the hottest, most barren part of the desert, they discovered that a great sandstorm had passed that way, covering everything in a carpet of fine brown earth. The markers were all hidden, and no one could find their ostrich eggs any more. So they walked and they walked, and each day the sun blazed more warm.

One morning, Xam saw in the distance the scraggly arms and branches of a baobab tree. It was his baobab tree. He trotted across the hot sands and knelt at its foot and dug and dug until he found the great big egg he had brought from home. But when he lifted the egg, he noticed that it was lighter than it had been before. Soon he realised why: his plug of stick and animal hide had worked its way loose, and all the water had spilled from the egg and run out into the fine desert sand.

I am guessing this has happened to you. It has happened to me. Haven't we all, at some time or another, failed to chew the piece of animal hide long enough to properly soften it, so that it falls out of our ostrich egg at the worst possible moment? I think we have. But wait – this is the important bit. Watch and see how Xam handles the situation.

Xam was unhappy at finding no water, but he didn't want his companions to mock him and slap him around more than they already had. So he carefully replaced the plug of stick and animal hide, and carried the egg back to the others. They all looked at him, expecting him to throw back his head and suck on the egg, but instead he just tucked it under his arm and, saying nothing, fell in step beside them.

And so they walked, and the others kept watching Xam out of the corners of their eyes, waiting for him to take a sip. But he never did. Occasionally he would shift the egg from one arm to the other, as though the weight were becoming too much, but he never said a word and he never took a sip.

And the others began to wonder at this. They wondered: Why isn't he drinking from that great big ostrich egg? And one said: "Maybe he knows something we don't. Maybe he knows that we are far from home without any water, and he will need that ostrich egg to get him home safely across the wide wastes of the desert."

And another said: "Maybe he is being noble. Maybe he is refusing to drink his water while we go thirsty."

And another said: "Maybe he is waiting to share his water with us when we all need it most."

And all of them were thinking: "Maybe if I am nice to him, he will give me some of that water. I want some of that water."

And so they began to behave differently towards Xam. They

started speaking to him again, and sharing their morsels of dried antelope meat, and they helped him catch lizards and scorpions and squeeze the moisture from them. And one of the older boys said: "When we get home how would you like to date my sister? She's a lot younger than she looks."

They wondered: Why isn't he drinking from that great big ostrich egg? And one said: "Maybe he knows something we don't."

They even offered to carry his ostrich egg for him, but Xam, sorry elephant tracker though he might be, was no fool and he always politely declined. And the more he kept silent, the more the others became convinced that he kept a mighty secret indeed.

And so by the time they reached home, the rest of the community noticed how the older boys hung on Xam's every word and click. They noticed how the older boys would share their food with him and offer to sweep away the hard rocks and little jagged bits of quartz before he lay down to sleep each night. They noticed these and many such things, and their respect for Xam grew. In due course and with the passing of time, Xam became the most respected and powerful man in the community.

Even the great Hide-and-Seek scandal of 72 – when nasty rumours circulated about Xam's loincloths having small rents in them, just the kind of rents you would expect to be made if someone took a sharp piece of flint and poked it forcefully against the animal hide, just the kind of rents that might make considerably simpler the astounding feat of tracking an ostrich across a gravel plain while blindfolded with your loincloth –

even this scandal did nothing to seriously threaten Xam's standing in the community.

And Xam lived long and died happy, or as happy as you can be when you're dying.

So what are we to learn from the story of Xam and the ostrich egg? If we but knew it, all the secrets of life are here. For one thing: you don't need to hunt your desert elephant to make a success of your life. No one needs to run with the bulls or harpoon Moby Dick or shag Mrs Dunstable to lead a fulfilled life – especially not shagging Mrs Dunstable, if what Gary Zephron told us after rugby practice behind the change-rooms is true. The truth is: you don't actually have to accomplish anything. All you need is to know how to fake it.

Inside us all there is the secret truth of ourselves – a truth that is hollow, like an eggshell that has spilt its water. We just need to embrace that hollowness, and give people the opportunity to persuade themselves that there is something there. Other people – never forget – are even more insecure and self-doubting than we are. They will fill in the secret for you. If you can pull that off, it doesn't matter how good or bad you are at anything else. I'm telling you, people, this is the way we want to go: we all need to find our inner ostrich egg.

We just need to embrace that hollowness, and give people the opportunity to persuade themselves that there is something there.

3

Finding Your Mate

The inner ostrich egg can help us in many situations. Consider love. Or if not love, that hot itchy feeling we tell our partners is love. Everybody wants love, or at least something to make that hot feeling stop itching. Love, indeed, is a many-splendoured thing.

(As opposed to whiskey, which is a many-blended thing. Love, on the whole, beats whiskey because, um … hang on a minute, I had it written down here somewhere. Oh yes – with whiskey you can sometimes run out of ice, and then you have to go next door and borrow some ice, but sometimes you forget how late it is, because time has no meaning when you are spending quality time with your whiskey, so you thoughtlessly wake up the neighbours and then they shout at you and tell you to bring back that copy of the Sunday newspaper they saw you stealing from their postbox, and then you threaten to burn their house down – because whiskey, bless her fickle charms, sometimes causes you to get your dander up – and then before you know it, things have gotten out of hand. Love does none of these things. Well, some of those things, but it seldom causes your neighbour to shout, unless you are loving too loudly while he is trying to watch the Miss Universe pageant on the television.)

At any rate, love is good. All the great ones have spoken highly of it. Especially Shakespeare – he was particularly lavish in his praise. Love, he said, is like a red, red nose. Or perhaps I am thinking of someone else. Anyway, at its best, love has many benefical side effects. It discourages us from taking that extra martini before hitting the road; it causes us to brush our teeth before going to bed; sometimes it helps us make slightly less of a fool of ourself at the office Christmas party. Plus, the scientists tell us, being in love causes our cholesterol levels to drop. In my experience, that is usually because my loved ones won't let me eat fillet steaks with a zesty blue-cheese sauce for breakfast any more, but still …

Love helps us make slightly less of a fool of ourself at the office Christmas party.

(On the down side, love has inspired many of the songs of Celine Dion and most of the public utterances of Michael Jackson, as well as giving rise to divorce lawyers, the suburbs and Valentine's Day. But let us not dwell on the negative.)

The big problem with love is the eternal snag of actually finding someone who will let you lie on top of them and whisper your lovin' mouthfuls in their ear. This has ever been the problem. It is tough enough for women, who traditionally have had to be locked in medieval towers or stand around in front of dragons' caves or dance in strip clubs while waiting for a knight errant or a wealthy Malaysian businessman to find them and carry them away, but it is no picnic for men either, especially those of us who are not knights errant or wealthy Malaysian businessmen. I, for one, am neither a knight errant nor a wealthy Malaysian businessman, and if you are anything like me – and I think you are – neither are you.

(I confess, this chapter is dedicated largely to the men of the world, but you ladies may want to read it too. Because if you don't, if you skip it and head straight on to the next section, you will finish your book before your partner – who hopefully is lying beside you reading his own personal copy – has even started the final chapter. This book has been carefully measured for a simultaneous finish – I find it more intimate that way – but if you should choose the headstrong, independent route, I can only ask that you don't spoil the surprise ending for him.)

When it comes to finding a mate, there has been much advice bandied about over the years, some of it useful.

"Get yourself a good club and some interesting wall-paintings, and for God's sake move out of your parents' cave, already," they told Australopithecus man.

"Get yourself a feudal barony and a village full of loyal peasants who have sworn an oath of vassalage, and whose brides you can sleep with on their wedding nights," they told medieval man.

(Incidentally, I have always wanted to wear an aftershave called *Droit de Seigneur*. And I would, only I don't think anyone makes an aftershave called *Droit de Seigneur*.)

"Get yourself a job, a car and a dark-blue suit," they told men in the 1950s.

"Get yourself some long hair and drugs," they told men in the 1960s. (In fact, that drug thing holds true for almost any era between now and forever.)

"Get yourself some dance moves, some dangling neck-jewellery, some assorted varieties of facial hair including sideburns, and a shirt made from a flammable synthetic material," they told men in the 1970s. "Oh," they added, "and don't forget the drugs."

"Get yourself a fax machine, a cordless telephone, a gym membership, a job you can't really explain to anyone in a way that would make sense, a car you can't afford and, of course, some drugs," they told men in the 1980s. In fact, let's just take that "car you can't afford" as read from now on as well.

"Get yourself a subscription to a glossy women's magazine, your own reflexologist, a private gym instructor, a set of face-care products created especially for men, a career that fulfils you, a creative outlet, a cellphone that you don't always feel the need to answer, the ability to cook at least three dishes that don't involve pasta or toast, one or more experiments in quirky facial hair, and a drug dealer who delivers to you," they told men in the 1990s.

You will notice that the must-have lists have steadily increased over the years. This is not because women have become noticeably more demanding of their men. Indeed, when you look at some of the villains and rotters and generally misshapen detrimentals you see walking about with beautiful women on their arms, you will share my suspicion that women demand almost no standards at all of the men they inexplicably select. No, the list of demands has grown because these are the demands we are putting on ourselves, damn our sorry eyes.

We are the ones who started saying: "Ooh, you've been right all these years: we *are* shallow, simple, one-dimensional beings. We *do* need to add colour to our wardrobe and depth to our lifestyles, in order best to bring out the goddess that is you. Look at me, I am cooking with capers and something that involves the word 'balsamic' in its name, and yet I am still earning a good salary and going to gym to make my stomach flat! Check it out, I can discuss feng shui, and almost pronounce it correctly! Love me, for I have opinions about interior decoration! See how multidimensional I am! Plus, can I read your copy of *Conversations with God* when you're finished?"

And women went: "Golly." Because they never expected us to believe all of that. They didn't even really believe it themselves. It was just an age-old ritual that we all followed, the same way that men don't always mind stopping and asking for directions – we just feel we have to pretend we do. But of course when confronted with this sudden mass offer to unilaterally disarm, women said: "Okay, dandy."

They would have been fools if they hadn't, and of the vast number of things that women are not, fools is right at the top of the list.

It would have been like the Russkis phoning up Reagan in the 80s and saying: "Comrade, we have thought about it, and we have decided that keeping these missile systems and nuclear warheads is more trouble than it's worth. We are going to dismantle them, and drop the parts in the sea near New Zealand. Unless, of course, you have some use for them? We could send our warheads directly over in the next mail, if you like? Carefully swaddled in bubble-wrap, of course, ha ha. You can add them to your arsenal. We'll even pay for the postage. And we'll stop drinking vodka, if you think that would be best?"

And Reagan thinking about it and going: "Nah, no need for that, pardners. I'd miss having another superpower around. Besides, there are so many areas of our relationship we haven't even explored yet. I've been meaning to talk to you about chemical warfare for a while now, and maybe this is the right time."

So you can't blame them for accepting the offer, but it has resulted in no good for any of us. Because here's the thing: *it doesn't work*. It certainly doesn't work for men: it is too much effort to improve yourself, especially when deep down your every Y chromosome is yelling out: "This is not an improvement! You were a better man when you had never used an olive-oil atomiser! You were a better man when you thought reiki was an oriental technique for gathering up loose leaves!"

It is too much effort, and you generally fail at it, which leaves you feeling like a failure, which is never any good for your sex life. And even if you get it right, the rewards are hardly worth the trouble. We become miserable and unmanly and we sublimate our desires in other, even less attractive ways.

So instead of spending all Saturday watching rugby, you spend all Sunday watching Formula One motor-racing, and then you pretend you are satisfied.

You were a better man when you thought reiki was an oriental technique for gathering up loose leaves.

Instead of saying, "I don't feel like talking about our relationship", you say: "I really want to talk about our relationship, but my bio-rhythmic chart suggests that I am experiencing an emotional peak right now, and I don't want to cloud what can be such a positive, life-enhancing experience with a tantrum that might lead to my walking out and drinking heavily at a strip club."

And women aren't any happier either. Women, God help them, *like* men. They have liked us for years, for centuries – forever, in fact – just as we were. I can't understand it any more than you can. It is one of those facts of life, like how a television works, or whether red and green traffic lights at opposing intersections really are always perfectly synchronised, that just has to be taken as an article of faith. If we stop to question it, chaos ensues. And that is precisely what we have done. We have questioned it. We have set out to be better.

(Which returns me to a theme: do not set out to be better. It isn't worth it.)

And now we are not the men that women have learned to resentfully love and lovingly resent, and that means women are as confused and listless as we are. It is even worse for them, because they have finally got what they want, and *it isn't what they want!* They are sitting there thinking: do I really, in the deepest part of me, want to share my life with someone who cares so much about whether Ally McBeal could ever have found true love with Robert Downey Jr? Wouldn't I maybe, secretly, rather be spending the night with Robert Downey Jr? Sure, he takes a lot of drugs and he'd never be home much, but in a weird sort of way, that's kinda sexy.

That is why my advice to the men of the new millennium is simple and pared down, like Norwegian furniture. (And how I wish that the reference to Norwegian furniture were not one that the men of new millennium would be so likely to understand.) It is this: find your inner ostrich egg.

That's it: find your inner ostrich egg.

I realise that you are new at this; you may need more. Remember Xam and his empty ostrich egg? Remember how when he clutched it to himself the others all wondered what his secret was? Remember how they all assumed that he had a secret at all? If the ostrich egg had been filled with water, and Xam had drunk it, or shared it, or even wondered aloud what he should do with it, he would not have become the most powerful man in his tribe. A secret is only powerful when it is still a secret.

That ostrich egg is inside us all, and if we cherish it, and cradle it, and refuse under any circumstances to explore its inner parts, then others will begin to imagine for themselves what is inside it. Women in particular prefer their own imaginings of who we are – and quite right too, since what they can imagine is infinitely more interesting and attractive than what is really the case.

So heed what I am saying: instead of trying to improve yourself, reap the benefits of letting others do the improvements for you. Make silence your friend. Cultivate the knowing look, the mysterious smile, the sudden unexplained frown, as though you were remembering words spoken a long time ago by someone very different. As long as you aren't sitting there slack-jawed and drooling, and as long as you don't keep laughing at all of their jokes, even the ones they don't find funny themselves, they will begin to sense depths and dimensions in you that you could scarcely have imagined, let alone conjured up by some misguided programme of self-betterment.

Instead of trying to improve yourself, reap the benefits of letting others do the improvements for you.

Let me share with you an anecdote to illustrate the perils of talking too much. My friend Chunko is eternally the optimist when it comes to meeting women. What's more, he is enterprising. He has spent the best years of his life hanging around laundromats and bowling alleys in the hope of finding an eligible young lady. (Why bowling alleys, you ask? Don't ask me. Chunko may be enterprising, but that doesn't make him smart.)

Last year he put in long hours at his local bookstore, to no avail. "No woman ever browses at the flyfishing department," he grumbled, "and if you hang around the self-help books, you're only going to meet the kind of woman who reads self-help books."

His most recent wheeze was supermarkets. I scoffed, but he was persuasive. “If you come with me,” he said, “I’ll buy the next round.”

Our first port of call was the local supermarket on a Sunday morning. “What we need to do,” said Chunko, “is refine some approach lines.”

I positioned myself at the fresh-produce department. Fruit and vegetables, I fondly imagined, offer a wealth of approach lines. Soon enough, a likely candidate approached. She seemed presentable and her hair had recently been washed. As I lingered, she fingered an avocado, and seemed to smile at me in an encouraging fashion. I thanked my stars. Avocados are approach lines waiting to happen.

Sauntering closer, I murmured: “Equal volumes of all gases contain the same number of molecules at the same temperature and pressure.” She looked at me levelly, and the warmth in her eyes cooled.

“I think you are mistaken,” she said. “I think you are trying to use an approach line regarding the avocado, a pear-shaped tropical fruit with a leathery green skin, large seed and edible pulp. Instead you are reciting Avogadro’s Rule, an hypothesis named after its originator, the eighteenth-century physicist Amego Avogadro.”

How do you think I should have responded to that situation? Do you think I should have smiled mysteriously, bowed courteously and withdrawn, leaving the subject to ponder whether I really was making a point involving the constituent properties of gases? Or do you think I should have stood there stammering, saying something along the lines of: "Oh, um, no, I was actually just thinking aloud, and, uh, uh, did he really live in the eighteenth century? I didn't know that …"

I leave it to you to guess which option I selected. I am simply the writer of this book; I don't always learn from it. My small consolation – and it is meagre indeed – is that over at the refrigerated section, Chunko was faring no better. He hovered beside the frozen poultry, leering at a severe-looking woman wearing no make-up. As she reached for the drumsticks, he contrived to lean forward so that their hands met above the braai packs.

The severe-looking woman withdrew her hand sharply. "Um …" said Chunko, "ummm …" Sympathetically, the woman offered him an escape. Holding out a packet of frozen fowl, she said: "Chicken breasts?"

A happy smile broke across Chunko's face. I grew cold, but there was nothing I could do. Chunko has never been very good at holding his silence. "No, not at all," he said, staring at the front of her T-shirt, "I think they're very attractive."

MAINTAINING THE MATE

Looking back, I can see now that that anecdote didn't really illustrate much at all. Never mind, too late now. At any rate, if you play your cards right and follow my advice, you will find that before long you have managed to snare yourself a love-partner. Do not relax, my brothers. Harder than winning is holding. Reach inside. Feel the smooth curve of your ostrich egg. Tap it. Hear how it echoes.

Avoid bringing new lovers to your home too soon. I don't

mean never let them see where you live – that is inviting them to imagine severed heads in your freezer and a small pile of hands in your crisper drawer. Or, worse, a wife.

But when you do bring them home, make sure everything is neatened up and tidied away. If you must have personal effects as decoration, make sure they are either suitably enigmatic, like a collection of live Venus Flytraps or a stuffed monitor lizard, or teasingly impersonal, like a chess set carved from narwhal ivory.

Be sure to take down your mounted collection of empty beer cans from around the world, or your very humorous mirror with the joke laws of cricket printed across it, or the five-litre beer mug with "My New Year's resolution is that I'll cut down to one drink a day" written on the side. Ditto any photographs of you and your friends taken:

a) during a fishing expedition
b) at your mate Kevin's stag party, especially if you have to point yourself out as being "the one with the bucket on my head"
c) at any occasion at which you happen to be wearing short pants. Unless you are raising the Rugby World Cup in triumph with Nelson Mandela patting you on the shoulder, avoid visual representations of yourself in short pants.

It is, however, acceptable to leave visible a framed photograph of yourself receiving the Academy Award or the Nobel Peace Prize, especially if it is turned slightly towards the wall to suggest modesty, and especially if you respond to her query by saying, "Oh that", and shrugging with a distantly amused smile playing at your lips. But only if you have really won an Academy Award or the Nobel Peace Prize. None of those hilarious fake newspaper front-pages saying "[Insert name here] wins Grand Prix of belching" or anything like that.

Unless you are raising the Rugby World Cup in triumph with Nelson Mandela patting you on the shoulder, avoid visual representations of yourself in short pants.

Besides, silence and mystery is cool. I would go so far as to say it constitutes coolth. Consider silent men: Steve McQueen, that James Bond villain with steel teeth, The Undertaker on WWF wrestling. Now consider talkative men: Woody Allen, Murray Walker, that guy at the office who likes to discuss how the next *Star Wars* movie is going to explore Darth Vader's descent into the dark side. Are you getting the point I am trying to make here?

Play it smart. When she says: "What are you thinking about?" – and you know she will – consider your response well.

Don't say: "I was wondering what you were thinking about." That is sad, and not at all mysterious.

Don't say: "I was thinking about how much I love you", because this is not only untrue but also devalues one of the last cards you have left to play. One day you will need that card to get out of a mess of sticky trouble, my friend, and you will be grateful you still have it up your sleeve.

You might get away with saying: "I was thinking about

how much I want to rip off your clothes with my teeth and get down to some serious carpet-aardvarking with you", but be careful what you wish for.

I would also counsel against honesty here. "I was thinking about what time the game starts on Saturday" or "I was wondering what is making that clinking noise in my engine whenever I drive above a hundred and ten" is simply giving away too much of yourself. Keep it cagey. Don't answer directly. Instead look out of the window and say: "Isn't it odd to think that Mozart/Noah/Golda Meir looked up at the very same moon?"

Don't say: "I was thinking about how much I love you", because this is not only untrue but also devalues one of the last cards you have left to play.

Do not misunderstand: this is not going to fool her into thinking that you really were musing on the vagaries of time, the flesh and this ever-changing world. It doesn't matter. Understand clearly: she *doesn't want to know* what you're really thinking. She wants you to provide the blank canvas on which she can paint her deepest dreams of what you might be like. Say it with me, my friends: Embrace your inner ostrich egg.

4

Finding Your Inner Mayan

By now I think we are getting the hang of our inner ostrich eggs. It takes some practice, learning to handle your egg, but when you have mastered it the world lies open and glistening before you. But beware. There is danger ahead. There are those who have not learnt to embrace their inner emptiness. There are those who are so afraid of the egg within that they will stop at nothing to fill it up, and they are not fussy about the filling.

Be careful, my comrades. The unwary among us will have their ostrich eggs filled with gloop and guff, with flimflam and flapdoodle before they know what's happening. What am I talking about? I think you know what I am talking about. Walk to your nearest bookstore and take a gander at what is on the shelves. Everywhere you turn there is some new line of hokum and bunkum just waiting to flow into us, like harbour water into a discarded beer can, were we but to give it a chance.

Each season it is something new. Just recently it was feng shui. Think about that: the big craze of the last while was a range of small and poorly edited books teaching us that our lives will be better if we start arranging our furniture the way they do in China. Now come on. If you were writing a jokey book about the kind of nonsense that people believe these days, you wouldn't be able to make that stuff up.

Everywhere you turned, people were hanging mirrors in their hallway, or taking mirrors down from the hallway, I forget which. I met a woman who covered the edges of her coffee table with small blobs of putty because – and I am not making this up – "it makes the corners rounded, which enables the energy to flow freely through the house". If there is energy flowing freely through your house, you need an electrician, or an exorcist, or a lightning conductor over your mantelpiece, not four blobs of grey-looking putty.

Besides, what makes the Far Easterners the great experts on achieving success through the wonders of interior design? I wonder if the Japanese Ministry of War had feng shui when the generals got together to cook up that grand Pearl Harbor idea. I wonder if Chairman Mao had arranged the right symmetry of water- features and light fittings when he sat up late of a night, sipping cocoa and scribbling down good ideas in his little red notebook:

If there is energy flowing freely through your house, you need an electrician, or an exorcist.

1. Send all intellectuals to work in paddy fields.
2. Beat them up, while we're about it.
3. Put up posters of me.

4. Remember to check that sofa is aligned parallel to lei lines. Or should that be perpendicular? I forget which.
5. Fetch an intellectual from the paddy fields to write down the principles of sofa-alignment, so I don't forget next time.
6. Shoot intellectual in head so that no one knows more about sofa-alignment than me.

Besides, things are different over there. What works for a Japanese pagoda, say, may not work quite as well for an upmarket townhouse. And take it from me, you don't want to start building your house like a Japanese pagoda. Have you seen the size of those places? You'll be forever banging your forehead on the lintel, and leaning against a wall and falling outside because the wall was made of paper. And a national taste for furniture that leaves no room for the La-Z-Boy genuine leatherette recliner, with collapsible mug-holder and twice-padded footrest, need expect no favours from me.

You would have thought we would have learnt our lesson from that whole koi-pond phase, but no. And while I'm on the subject, the next person who looks at me disparagingly when I push aside the chopsticks at an oriental restaurant is going to have a lot more on his plate than he ordered. I'm not going to say this again: the reason we eat with forks is that we long ago discovered that four sharp prongs offer a more efficient means of manipulating food than do two bits of blunt stick. I am not being backward when I eat with a fork – I am using modern technology, damn it.

But enough of that. There are many such egg-fillers about. I encountered another one just the other day. I was slinking through my local bookstore – perhaps the very store in which you bought this book – when I was accosted by a young lady waving a glossy paperback.

"Have you read this?" she enthused with a voice like loose change falling from your pocket and rolling down the pavement. "It will change your life. It contains the lost wisdom of the ancient Mayans." The book was called *The Avocado Prophecies* or *Footprints of the Toucans* or some such flummery. I clucked and tutted and fixed her with a stern eye. I have no patience with Loser Chic.

The next person who looks at me disparagingly when I push aside the chopsticks at an oriental restaurant is going to have a lot more on his plate than he ordered.

LOSER CHIC

Loser Chic is what I call our modern obsession with celebrating the losers of pre-history. Any hodgepodge of antiquated mysticism is celebrated nowadays, provided it can be attributed to the Incas or the Etruscans or any other culture that has disappeared from the face of the earth with scarcely a trace. I don't get it. Whatever misty romance these people may offer, the fact of the matter is: they lost. In the big boardgame of history, they threw the losing dice.

Tell me, besides pioneering communal cocaine use and celebrating the social merits of human sacrifice, what can the Inca teach us? How to be invaded by a rag-tag bunch of unshaven Spaniards? If those ancient civilisations were so damned clever, where are they now? Eh? Building pyramids in the jungle is all very well, but they might have found the wheel a touch more useful in the long run.

> **Whatever misty romance these people may offer, the fact of the matter is: they lost. In the big boardgame of history, they threw the losing dice.**

(I accept, as I must, that history is long and that one day Fortuna's wheel will turn and Western culture – however you might conceive it will one day be eclipsed by the resurgent communities of Burundi or Papua New Guinea. I accept that, and when it happens I won't expect the triumphant Papua New Guineans to write nostalgic books reminiscing about how the early twenty-first-century West invented Reality Television and expressed their aspirations through the artistic career of Christina Aguilera.)

The current Losers *du Jour* are the Mayans. You can't drink a cappuccino in your local bookstore these days without spilling your foam on another meaty tome celebrating the arcane knowledge and buried insights of the noble Mayans (or Maya, you might prefer to call them). Ooh, how clever they were, and how communal their lifestyle. What lovely buildings they built. Plus, what sharp timekeepers they were – did you know, they built sundials and they knew the movement of the stars?

Well, of course they knew the movement of the stars!

What else are you going to do at night if you're a Mayan? Watch TV? Read a book?

The Mayans are especially popular at the moment, because the Mayans predicted the world would come to an end on Sunday, 23 December 2012 – coincidentally, precisely the day my endowment policy matures. But enough about me. After the slight disappointment of the year 2000 and Nostradamus and the new millennium and all, and the fact that Table Mountain didn't reveal itself to be a flat-topped pyramid that was actually a spaceship that would gather together the spiritually enlightened and take them up to Betelgeuse, the spiritual conspiracy-theorists have been casting about for another big occasion.

The Mayans have given us 2012, and so 2012 is already shaping up to be the next big communal boo-hoo and brouhaha. And if the Mayans predicted 2012 – no matter that almost everything else they did failed and crumbled back into the jungle – then the Mayans must be a smart bunch of cookies.

And so we are beset on all sides by chattering voices urging us to reach inside and find the lost wisdom of the Maya, to find the Mayan within. Do not listen, my children. It is a trick to fill your eggshell. More than that – it is just plain dumb. Always remember: we may be lazy, but we are not dumb. It is only the very smart who can get away with being as lazy as we are.

Let's have another look at these fabulous Mayans, shall we? Let's take a closer peek at these models of wisdom and insight. The Mayans, it turns out, had a vibrant sporting culture, similar to our own. Nothing wrong there. They were fond of a particular ball sport, the rules of which are sadly lost to us, mainly because the Mayans didn't know how to write in a language we can understand. I have a sneaking suspicion that they weren't that big on rules either.

We may be lazy, but we are not dumb. It is only the very smart who can get away with being as lazy as we are.

On special days, the city would gather round to watch the game, at the conclusion of which the winning team were given a rubdown and a chew of coca leaves, and the losing team were given a sympathetic handshake and put to death. Again, details of the actual execution are sketchy, but there is strong evidence to suggest that part of the winning team's winnings was the privilege of consuming the still-beating hearts of the losers. History, alas, doesn't record what happened to the coach of the losing team.

No harm done, you might think. We could stand to encourage a little more of the winning culture among our own sportsmen and business executives. Perhaps so, but read on.

An even more impressive recreational activity was the Mayan enthusiasm for sustained bouts of heavy drinking. With the combination of ingenuity and far-sightedness for which they are today rightly celebrated, they solved the vexing problem of how to continue drinking after the body has had enough.

Once the vomiting mechanism had kicked in – nowadays

a sign to all but the most hard-working member of parliament that it is time to leave the party – they simply whipped out their banana-leaf funnels and continued taking their favourite tipple as an enema. Hence, I suppose, the old Mayan drinking salute, "Bottoms up".

(As an historical aside, the old Mayan drinking salute is one of only two authentic Mayan expressions in common use today. The other comes down to us from the prenuptial contract of the first marriage of a Mayan woman to a man from the non-Mayan world. Negotiations were tough, and involved drinking. The contract was prolix, but could be summarised as follows: "What's Mayan is Mayan, and what's yours is also Mayan.")

So what are we to make of these anthropological facts? What kind of people do the self-helpers expect us to emulate? Murderous sports thugs with a pathological compulsion to drink, that's what. Well, I have news for you. There are communities of modern-day Mayans all around us. They are called university residences. I lived in one such community for two years, and I wish you could hear the quaver in my voice and see the purple fear in my eyes when I tell you that I don't want to go back.

Let me tell you something else about the Mayans. One day, after several thousand years of more-or-less civilisation, they all just upped and abandoned their cities. They gobbled down their last heart, packed away their banana leaves and walked into the jungle, never to return.

Many theories have been advanced to account for this mass abandonment, including a breakdown of traditional hierarchies of faith and authority, combined with the threat of external invasion. I don't think so. If you ask me, it wasn't the fear of attack from outside that made the Maya leave – they were just tired of being Mayans. And after what we have heard today, who could blame them? It wasn't the enemy without that destroyed their civilisation; it was the enema within.

My advice on finding your inner Mayan is this: Don't bother. He will find you when he needs to borrow some money.

NONSENSICAL CHIC

It isn't just Loser Chic that is in vogue. Do not underestimate the determination of the self-helpers and money-spinners to sell you something to fill that inner ostrich egg. They know that most of what they are selling makes no sense, so they make a virtue of how little sense it makes.

"Every woman is a goddess," a woman said to me recently. She looked at me with that haughty look that goddesses have. Actually, it was more like the haughty look that llamas have, but I let it pass. She had just been reading a book titled *Women Who Run with the Voles While They Wait for the Wolves to Return Their Call.* (No, she hadn't. I just made that up because I wanted to use the word "voles".)

"But if every woman is a goddess," I said slowly, so that I could understand, "then what exactly does it mean to be a goddess? Doesn't it just mean being like every other woman? Surely the word 'goddess' then has no special meaning? If every woman is a goddess, why not just go on calling yourselves women?"

"You are applying masculine thought processes to a phenomenal experience," said the goddess. I didn't know quite how phenomenal I was finding the experience, but I plugged ahead.

"So surely there must be some room for improvement in this world of goddessness, otherwise what's the point of all the self-help books you read?" I persisted, feeling a headache coming on. "Are there different levels of goddess? Like, are there maybe normal goddesses, and then someone like you is an advanced goddess?"

She gave a small toss of her head. "Clearly," she said, "you do not understand non-rational wisdom."

Now that is the kind of person with whom you do not want to have a conversation. If Neale Donald Walsch had written *Conversations with a Goddess*, and had selected her, he would have sold about four copies. The book would have been no worse than *Conversations with God*, mind you, but then it is not quality that sells self-help books. I hope.

My point is that they are celebrating the nonsense of things that make no sense. I don't know if you've ever read a book called *All I Really Need to Know I Learned in Kindergarten*. I really hope you haven't. Some dolt named Robert Fulghum used an entire forest of trees to rhapsodise about the emotional appeal of Crayola crayons, and draw life lessons and inspiration from – I am not kidding – the exploits of the Eensy Weensy Spider.

He couldn't be making it more clear: if you read self-help books, he was saying, I can tell you the kind of thing I would tell a four-year-old, and you will be content. The only difference between you and a four-year-old is that you will shell out your hard-earned cash to buy my book.

I don't even want to start talking about that other chucklehead, Deepak Chopra. When I first heard Deepak Chopra's name, I thought he was a Los Angeles gangsta rapper. Then I read one of his books, and I realised that stacked up against Deepak Chopra, the life's work of Tupac Shakur is a model of good sense, sound advice and lyrical beauty. I don't like to make fun of my fellow writers, but that's okay, because Deepak Chopra isn't a fellow writer. Deepak Chopra isn't a writer's cuticle.

Consider this limpid puddle of prose: "But now a stage comes when the seeker is born into the seer. Because the seeker has discovered that that which the seeker was seeking was the seeker, and having sought the seeker, the seeker becomes the seer."

Not even the most ardent Chopraphiliac can pretend to enjoy something like that.

Or think of this: "The only difference between you and tree", says the perceptive Chopra, "is the informational and energy content of your respective bodies."

That is also the only difference between me, a tree and George W. Bush. Hang about – no, that is not the only difference. A tree has leaves, damn it, and sucks up water from the ground, and lets dogs urinate against it. And George W. Bush … actually, I suppose George W. Bush is a little like a tree. Oh, I can't think any more. When I read too much Deepak, I have to reach for my six-pack.

Now do you understand why it is so hard to write a book that tries to satirise self-help books? When it comes to the self-help genre, the line between satire and the real thing is drawn in water with a blunt pencil.

5
Who Moved My Keys?

By now you are no doubt turning to your partner, who is I trust lying in bed beside you with his or her own personal copy of *I Moved Your Cheese*, and asking: "Say, why is this book called *I Moved Your Cheese*? I haven't seen much sign of cheese, and why would anyone want to move it anyway? What gives?"

The answer is not, as certain cynics and sceptics have already cruelly suggested within earshot, that we are hoping by a cheap ruse to cash in on the popularity of a recent best-selling book in the self-help genre. Not at all. The answer to your question will, I hope, become clear in due course. Just give that Osmatix™ time to work.

Meanwhile, I would like to offer some words of counsel on the subject of coping with change. Coping with change is a hot topic at the moment, and I think I understand your anxieties. If you are anything like me – and if you have read this far, I think you are – the kind of change that most disturbs and annoys you is one that each morning causes you to throw back your head and bellow: "*Who moved my keys?*"

Because let's be honest with ourselves: we are not much concerned with the big changes. Your company, which once specialised in manufacturing hula-hoops specifically designed for left-handed people, is being pressured by market forces to diversify into making security gates? Well boo-hoo. You either roll with it or you stay at home and become an alcoholic and watch *Days of Our Lives* until you remember that you have always wanted to become a fashion designer or maybe a porn star. That is your destiny, and unless you are an utter dunderhead with no capacity to think more than five minutes ahead – and I am confident that you are not – there is nothing that anyone can tell you that will make very much difference.

But it is not the big things that cause the real stress. It is the little things, like dashing for the door to beat the morning rush-hour traffic and discovering – wouldn't you know it? – that someone has moved your keys again. Seriously, it happens all the time. I put my keys down where I can be sure to find them – like in the pocket of the trousers I was wearing yesterday, or between the cushions on the couch or, if I have worked really late the night before, in the freezer section of the refrigerator, next to the ice-trays – and in the morning, without fail, I can never find them again. Someone has moved my keys!

This causes stress. What causes even more stress is when my partner says: "I've told you a hundred times to hang the keys up on the hook for the keys. Then you will always know where they are when you're trying to leave."

And of course I have to say, "I don't have a hook for keys.

Have you ever seen a hook for keys? No, that's because I don't have one."

And then she will say: "Well, you should have one. Anyway, look at me; I never have any trouble finding my keys."

Then that causes me to take even longer to leave, because of course now, besides finding my own keys, I have to surreptitiously look for my partner's keys, and hide them somewhere she won't easily find them, without her noticing that I am doing it. That's right: I move her keys.

(It is, of course, a useless plan. Women have a supernatural gift not given to men. Women can find things you have lost with barely a blink or a scratch, the way a drug-sniffer dog at an international airport can find biltong in your backpack, or the way a Cape Town waiter can without hesitation pick out the sole out-of-towner in a party of eight and unerringly bring him the wrong order.)

It is no good telling me, as well you might, that I shouldn't sweat the small stuff. Sweating the small stuff is what makes us function normally. If we didn't get depressed that our team lost the cricket on Saturday, we would have all that capacity for depression just lying around, waiting to attach itself to something big, like global warming or the commercial hunting of minke whales or the ongoing commercial success of Eminem.

It is no good telling me that I shouldn't sweat the small stuff. Sweating the small stuff is what makes us function normally.

If my partner weren't sitting with her girlfriends on a

Saturday morning, drinking cappuccino and saying: "And you know what I can't stand? I can't stand the way he never puts his keys down in the same place when he gets home", she would be freed up to be saying: "And you know what I can't stand? I can't stand the way he always goes out in the morning, pretending he has a job, when really I know that he goes down to the Chalk 'n Cue and wins money from people who bet that he can't sing the theme song to *Ally McBeal* while simultaneously smoking a cigarette and downing a tankard of beer."

But of course, the keys are not necessarily keys. They might also be one half of my pair of lucky green socks, or my cigarette lighter, or that last beer that I could have sworn I left in the crisper section of the refrigerator, cunningly hidden under the head of lettuce that has been there since 1998, but which I keep around especially for the purpose of hiding my last beer. For some reason, all of these things go missing too.

No matter. I say to you: Embrace the little irritations. Little irritations can be solved, and they keep your mind away from the big issues, which are just going to bog you down and depress you and about which you will never really be able to do anything meaningful.

But I realise that it is customary to offer these lessons in the form of useful parables. Let's say – and again I must emphasise that I am not thinking of any best-selling self-help book in particular here – that there are four little characters who live in a maze.

Two of them are mice, because mice live in mazes, and the other two are tiny little people, roughly the size of mice. That may seem unrealistic to you. Too bad. The little people and the mice are all very happy at the beginning of this parable, because they have a regular supply of cheese. Ah, cheese.

But then one day they wake up and discover that there is no more cheese. The two mice, being mice, head off into the maze and find some new cheese – although I suspect it was really the same old cheese that someone had moved to a different place. The two little people, being people, I suppose, sit around and complain and try to figure out what has happened to their cheese.

Now you might think that the moral of this story is: Embrace change; adapt yourself to the new circumstances of cheeselessness; go into the maze and find your cheese. But you would be wrong. That is the mouse's way of going about things.

Tell me, my brothers: are we mice or men? Because the real question is: who *did* move my keys? (Or, in the case of the parable, cheese?) Because if there *is* a serial cheese-mover on the loose, he or she is unlikely to stop at once. Having acquired the taste for moving cheese, there is nothing to stop them moving it again and again – and again, if they are not stopped – all the while snickering up their sleeve at your discomfort.

If you insist on scuttling after the cheese, you are inviting yourself into a world of hurt. Remember Xam and his desert elephant? Think of the desert elephant as the cheese. You could go trudging after that desert cheese all year, and when you found it you might still not know what to do with it. If you can't find your cheese, move on to something else.

Find something else that you can pretend is important. Pretending it is important will make it so. It is not the objective that counts, but your success in finding it. Enough with the cheese already.

Remember: objectives can be shifted; success can be manufactured. Anything can be faked.

But back to the parable. As I say, the little people's reaction was quite correct – the thing to do is to find out who did move your cheese. Because if you can find them, you can tie them up and poke them with sharp objects until they tell you where the cheese is. And then you can get them to go steal the mice's cheese and bring it to you.

If you can find who moved your cheese, you can tie them up and poke them with sharp objects until they tell you where the cheese is. And then you can get them to go steal the mice's cheese and bring it to you.

Which is why, whenever I can't find my keys in the morning and my partner is rattling on about how it is somehow my fault, I find it is a useful strategy to stand in the middle of the lounge yelling: "Who moved my keys? Damn it, did you move my keys?"

If you do that long enough, she will forget about blaming you and she will stalk through, take one look around the room and find your keys in the bottom of the fishtank, where you left them last night when you arrived home late, thoughtfully anticipating that in a glass-sided fishtank they would be in plain sight from anywhere in the lounge. Then she will point to them with a stern finger and say in a voice steeped and simmered with sarcasm: "Yes, that's right, Darrel. I moved your keys!"

I don't care. She can be as sarcastic as she likes. At least she has stopped blaming me. And even better: I have my keys!

Now that I have my keys and I have some time to think, I wonder if my mouse analogy was really all that helpful. Or even if it had anything to do with the point I was trying to make. Between you and me, I may not be all that good at this simple-minded-analogy business. Anyone who bought this book hoping for some help with coming to terms with being retrenched from the left-handed hula-hoop factory is probably going to be sitting there now tearing out the pages and using them as cocktail napkins or absorbent kitchen wipes. He's going to be calling up his other retrenched buddies and saying, "Say, have you fellows read *I Moved Your Cheese*? You have? What say we go over to that bastard's house and clean his clock for him? I'll bring the sandbags and the rubber gloves. What's that? Why am I talking in an American accent? Am I? Sorry, I hadn't noticed."

This is obviously not the defence I will use if several disgruntled out-of-work middle-management types come knocking on my door, but my opinion on the matter is simple: if you really need me or anyone else to spin you a feeble yarn with such electrifying insights as: "Change happens" and "You should adapt to change when it happens" and "If you don't move with change you will be left behind", then frankly you didn't deserve your job in the first place. And for the sake of the economy, you shouldn't be given another one.

This is my advice on coping with change: keep a small jar on the kitchen counter in which, each night when you get home, once you have hidden your keys, you deposit the larger of your loose coins. I suggest you donate small coppers to the needy or unload them on car guards. I often do that, which might explain why my car radio keeps getting stolen. My good friend Chunko keeps his spare change in an old rugby sock, which he keeps under his pillow for self-protection in the night. He needs it: Chunko's wife still hasn't forgiven him for trying to pick up severe-looking women in the supermarket.

Remember: change is inevitable, but unless you manage it well, it will make the coin section of your wallet stretch and will cause an unsightly bulge in your trousers.

6

Being and Nothingness

A great source of anxiety for young people making their way in the world today is the mindless advice that is regularly rolled out – like a length of artificial lawn – by professional advice-givers and well-meaning but misguided friends and relatives.

Advice is very much like the low-impact aerobic skiing machine you bought from a late-night infomercial – you hang on to it for a while, not really paying it much attention, then you pass it along to someone else. It is the only thing to do with advice and aerobic skiing machines, because you never actually use them yourself.

There is an awful lot of bad advice knocking about. For instance, there is that whole cultural reservoir of frankly puzzling hand-me-down wisdom that has been loitering about for centuries, being rightfully ignored then punted ahead like a rusted soup can for the next generation to pick up, ignore, then punt ahead in their turn.

Why, for instance, do we insist on declaring that a stitch in time saves nine, rather than, as recent studies seem to suggest, a number closer to seven-and-a-half? And what thinking parent would voluntarily tell their child that a watched pot never boils? That is the quickest way to shatter the myth of parental infallibility. All the little tyke needs is a pot, some water, a heat source and a pair of eyes, and soon he will know that you are all busk and bunkum, just like your parents before you.

Nor does the falsehood end there. Unless he is irretrievably drunk, he who laughs last, far from laughing longest, usually stops abruptly with an embarrassed look on his face. The next time you are tempted to solemnly intone that a rolling stone gathers no moss, take a gander at Keith Richards' teeth. What's more, I would be very surprised if the rain in Spain really does stay mainly on the plains. Does Spain even have plains? Bulls, yes, and haciendas, and women in red skirts, but I have never noticed any plains. Perhaps I have been looking in the wrong places.

The next time you are tempted to solemnly intone that a rolling stone gathers no moss, take a gander at Keith Richards' teeth.

I don't suppose it really matters what the meteorological profile of Spain is – unless of course you happen to be an itinerant Spanish umbrella salesman looking to unload your stock – but my point is that people throw around that sort of casual counsel with merry disregard for the truth. How many times has someone said to you: "Cheer up. Things can only get better"? This sort of bare-cheeked dishonesty is nothing short of insulting. If things have one common property upon which we can all agree, it is surely that they can always get worse. Given half a chance, things deteriorate faster than the second half of a Jim Carrey movie.

Another piece of advice that has me clucking and tutting at its sheer muddle-headed wrongness is the one that goes: "Always be yourself." Have you ever heard anything so appalling? Civilisation and all standards of human decency are precisely predicated on us *not* being ourselves. Haven't you ever read *Lord of the Flies*? Or tussled with another person for the last parking space at the mall? Underneath our glossy hairstyles, we are animals.

Even leaving aside the nature–nurture debate, being yourself is fraught with peril. Most of us, deep down, are sneaking, skulking, sometimes snivelling scaredy-cats, emotionally ambivalent, morally tenuous and possessed of a hidden liking for certain kinds of popular music that we would not under any circumstances reveal in public. Why should we be that person? In a world of people who seem rather more interesting than we are, why should we be stuck with ourselves? If being yourself were so great, there'd be queues of people wanting to be you.

What makes the advice worse is that it is usually being offered to someone who has conclusively demonstrated that themself is precisely the wrong person to be in that particular situation. If you have asked a girl to your matric dance and she has not only rejected you out of hand but insisted on singing a mocking song that rhymes aloud her opinion that you are not merely physically unattractive but also have a distasteful personality and many annoying habits, I think the message you should be getting is that if you want her to go to the dance with you, "yourself" is the very last thing you should continue to be.

Even worse is how people say "Be yourself" without so much as a moment's consideration of whom they are addressing. I am haunted by mental images of the young Jeffrey Dahmer approaching the school guidance counsellor with a couple of questions about certain troubling dreams he'd been having lately, and the counsellor nodding and frowning while really thinking about a beer and his afternoon nap, and telling him: "My best advice to you, young man, is to always be yourself."

So the crux of what I'm saying is: Don't feel you have to always be yourself. Be someone else if necessary. For instance, if you are Slobodan Milosevic, be someone who isn't a genocidal villain. If you are George W. Bush … but no, I promised myself no more George W. Bush jokes in this book.

I am not suggesting, mind, that you attempt to improve yourself. Oh no. That takes time and effort, almost invariably doesn't work, and still leaves you stuck with being you. Just be someone else for a while. This world is too varied to allow you to persist successfully with being only one person. "I am large," said Walt Whitman, "I contain multitudes." At least I think it was Walt Whitman. Or it might have been Goldfinger, in that scene where Sean Connery is strapped to the table with the laser beam.

If you are just a run-of-the-mill slob, with no special talents or burning interests, well, join the club. There are billions of us, with many more behind us and trillions still to come. In fact, it is my considered opinion that in the history of the world there have only been seven or eight unique or original people, and everyone else just tries to imitate one or more of them, with varying degrees of success. (I know you are expecting me to reveal who those people are, but I am too wily an author for that. I will say, however, that none of them is John Lennon. Or Shirley MacLaine. Or anyone with whom you or I are personally acquainted.)

If you have mastered the art of handling your ostrich egg, you will by now have realised that all things are possible. Which is to say: all things can be faked. You can be anyone you want to be.

BEING OPRAH

"You can be anyone you want to be." As I wrote those words I realised they sounded familiar. Then I remembered: I hear them on *Oprah* all the time. Oprah is fond of telling you that you can be anyone you want to be, no matter how poor, downtrodden or black-in-a-southern-state-of-the-USA you are. This is because, by telling you that, she is reminding you that she was once poor, downtrodden and black-in-a-southern-state-of-the-USA, but now she has more money than there are catfish in the Louisiana bayou.

In fact, to hear Oprah talk about it, you would think that she only escaped her childhood by buttering up her wrists, slipping them from the manacles and fleeing the chain-gang just before she and her sisters were loaded onto a paddle-steamer to be sold up the Mississippi, Simon Legree lashing at their bloodied shoulders with a rawhide bullwhip. I keep wanting to remind Oprah that she only acted in an Alice Walker story; she didn't actually live there.

Oprah has a segment on her show called "Remember your spirit". Now what on earth does that mean? Are you going to find yourself on a hiking trek in the mountains, going through your backpack in your tent in the evening, saying, "Let's see now, flashlight, waterproof matches, snake repellant, groundsheet … say, where's my spirit? Dang, I've forgotten my spirit again. WHO MOVED MY SPIRIT?!"

I keep wanting to remind Oprah that she only acted in an Alice Walker story; she didn't actually live there.

Are you going to find yourself facing the final question on *Who Wants to Be a Millionaire?*, with the host saying, "For a million bucks, Mavis, can you identify the immortal part of you that will live on after death?" And afterwards will you be walking away looking ashen, muttering over and over: "I can't believe I forgot my spirit. I can't believe I forgot my spirit"?

(Incidentally, I seem to remember that a few years ago South African Breweries had a campaign that involved placing signs in bottlestores that read: "Don't forget the beer." I'm not pointing any fingers, but I think someone might owe someone royalties.)

But you have to hand it to Oprah: she handles her inner ostrich egg like a champ. See how she keeps a straight face while she informs a universe of unhappy homebodies that they, with a little faith, could be her. That's right, honey – if you follow your bliss you too could be sitting up there next to Oprah, chatting to Denzel Washington and Maria Shriver and Gary Zukav and that bald-headed marriage counsellor whose name I have never bothered to remember.

That is what Oprah tells them, and she doesn't even blink when she says it. She looks them in the eye and tells them something that can't possibly be true, and they love her for it. Because no one can be Oprah. Because not even Oprah is Oprah. Oprah the phenomenon is just an idea whose time had come, and Oprah the person was just smart enough and sufficiently inert to let herself inhabit the idea, and to let the idea to take her shape.

No one can be Oprah. Because not even Oprah is Oprah. Oprah the person was just smart enough to let herself inhabit the idea.

Oprah doesn't bring her personality to the show, and she doesn't really have anything to talk to her celebrity guests about, besides casual references to other celebrity guests. She just billows in and lets the momentum of the idea that is Oprah take over. She becomes the ostrich egg, and allows a grateful audience to fill her up with whatever they prefer to imagine.

You too can be like Oprah, and I don't just mean by eating more banana cream pies and extra helpings of hominy grits than is strictly necessary. I mean you can let yourself flow as she flows. She doesn't appear to flow – she appears to just sit there like a silo – but she's flowing all right. She's flowing in a non-flowing kind of way, if that doesn't sound too much like Deepak Chopra.

(Hell, it does sound too much like Deepak Chopra. I have been reading too many self-help books. I'd better move along, and sharpish.)

Oprah embraces the egg, and although she appears to be an egg-filler and a guff-merchant, you can be sure that inside she is just as you and I would wish to be. When she's sitting up there, she's not thinking about angels and walking toward the light. She's thinking about who to hire to write her next self-help book, or about doing the carpet-aardvark with Shaquille O'Neal, or how to get Gary Zukav to sit up straight when he's on television, or buying a Lear jet so that the next time she flies somewhere she doesn't have to sit next to all those people who could be just like her. She tries to pretend otherwise, but we can see through her. And that is as it should be.

You know, just thinking about Oprah has made me hungry. I always associate Oprah with food, because I have a photograph of Oprah glued to my refrigerator door, along with a message, spelt out in those little magnetised letters that annoying people use to compose snatches of ghastly poetry.

I think they write that poetry to dissuade me from going into their fridges. There is nothing quite so distasteful as other people's idea of poetry. Although in this case I use the word "poetry" kindly. They are never really more than gloopy lyrical outbursts, or sticky snatches of pastel-coloured soft porn, four or five words long. I have to keep fighting the urge to grab these people by the collar and say: "Look, here is a pencil and paper. If you must write poetry, sit down and write it properly, not in the length of time it takes you to swig from the milk carton and scratch your belly. And when you have written your poetry on this piece of paper, put this paper in a drawer or a shoebox where unsuspecting visitors do not have to read it."

And then I also want to add: "And by the way, putting three words next to each other that all start with the same letter does not make it poetry."

But I am not talking about fridge-magnet poetry. I am talking about the message that is on my fridge underneath the photograph of Oprah. The message is this:

"Lard is no barrier to success, as long as you can fake it."

And that brings me to the subject of my next chapter.

7

The Body Beautiful

The body is always a ticklish subject. I have made no secret of my desire to lead the untroubled life, to avoid with strenuous rigour any temptation to rigorously strain myself, and yet like most of you reading this today, I am human. I am prone to petty vanity.

Just the other day, in an unguarded moment, I was prevailed upon to remove my shirt in mixed company. The circumstances aren't important, although I can reveal that they involved a deck of cards, a bucket of gin martinis, a small tub of tangy avocado dip and a toothbrush.

Without a scrap of the natural delicacy that causes men to fix a polite smile and avoid eye-contact when a porker presents herself in T-shirt and Bermudas, the women present made no secret of their horror. Their jaws fell open with an unattractive clicking sound. "I didn't know you drank so much beer," said one. "Shame, and you're not even forty yet," said another. A young mother hurried her small children from the scene, covering their eyes with her hands.

The sniggers continued throughout the cruel afternoon,

even after I had replaced the shirt and draped myself in a loose-fitting tablecloth. It was all very distressing. But here's the worst: like other men of my age and station, I have in the past been so shamed by such incidents that I have made rash decisions to do something about it.

Such resolutions usually begin in the gym. I am no fan of the gym. My idea of unnecessary physical exercise is eating at a buffet. Spinning is what happens after I arrive home late and discover I still have a bottle of grapefruit schnapps in the fridge. I have never yet had a conversation with a living person in a gym. People there are thinner and firmer than me, which intimidates me, and also makes me hate them. There are some people who are in worse shape than I am, I suppose, but who wants to talk to the fat kids?

I am no fan of the gym. Spinning is what happens after I arrive home late and discover I still have a bottle of grapefruit schnapps in the fridge.

I have toyed with the idea of home exercise, but not for very long. The thought of exerting myself in my own home makes a mockery of all that I hold dear, namely drinking beer on the couch. I don't even like to do home maintenance or odd-jobs. When the lightbulb in the bedroom burnt out, I pushed my bed into the kitchen and read by the little yellow refrigerator light for a month. It was comfortable enough, although I did once fall asleep without shutting the fridge door and woke with my eyes frozen shut and my tongue sticking to the bed-post.

(There may be those among you who question whether

pushing a bed into a kitchen might not have been slightly more arduous than changing a lightbulb. Perhaps, but you must realise that I was trying to make a point. There are no lengths to which I will not go to protect my slothfulness.)

Still, the home-exercise apparatus industry has ways of reaching out to you. To the blessed fact that I have not succumbed, I attribute more good fortune than strength of will. The standard home-exercise apparatus is marketed to you directly, via the late-night infomercial. I am especially susceptible to the siren song of the late-night infomercial, mainly because late-night is generally when I am at my most drunk.

The infomercials to which most of the world is treated are particularly compelling because they are American, and the Americans know how to sell. They adorn their infomercials with former Miss Americas and one-time gymnastic Olympic silver-medalists and current Dallas Cowboy cheerleaders and one-time day-time soapie stars and Suzanne Somers, formerly of *Three's Company* and that recent good-for-nothing sitcom with Patrick Duffy. You see these apple-cheeked beamers and you think to yourself: Golly, how blonde and pneumatic. How supple, despite her advanced age and obvious drug habit. And then you think: perhaps if I buy my very own set of titanium-bladed Ginsu knives, I too can live like a Californian.

I might well have fallen to the blandishments of the marketing arm of the home-exercise apparatus industry, had I not found myself with time on my hands late one night during a business trip to Amsterdam. I know what you are thinking, but unlike every other man with time on his hands late one night on a business trip to Amsterdam, I did not leave my hotel room. Instead I declared the mini bar open for business and flipped through the Dutch television stations. What do you think you might find after midnight on Dutch television? Would you have guessed that it would be an Italian infomercial for a home-exercise apparatus?

And then you think: perhaps if I buy my very own set of titanium-bladed Ginsu knives, I too can live like a Californian.

It was educational. Where South Africans rejoice in the glories of Verimark, the Italians embrace Tell-Sell. Where the Americans flog us the Alpine Skier and the Fitness Flyer – items of light-metal abstract art adorning many a walk-in closet around the nation – the Italians still touchingly put their faith in a product called Vibromass.

Vibromass is that machine, roundly forgotten in the rest of the world, which provides vibrating leather bands that encircle one's waist or thighs and shudder away cellulite and money. An elderly Italian woman talked us through the product, her hair the colour of saffron, her eyeliner so thick her face resembled a killer whale's. I don't mean to be ungallant, but she frightened me.

The elderly Italian lady looked properly excited to be on Dutch television at two in the morning, and expressed that excitement by beating a length of bamboo against the enormous buttocks of a young lady in a leotard.

I was face-to-cheeks with cultural difference. Where the

Americans shrewdly use the "After" model in their slimming-machine demonstrations, Italians evidently prefer the "Before". Unless of course – horrible thought – that young lady was the Italian idea of an "After" model. Either way, it made for tough viewing, especially late at night in a hotel room in a strange city, with the casual viewer not quite drunk enough to spend his unborn children's inheritance on the, er, pay-per-view channels.

"If you use the machine too much," cautioned the Italian crone atmospherically, as a leather band churned the model's lower hemispheres into a heaving Vesuvian mound of spandex and flesh, "you might feel pain." The lass was prevailed upon to arrange the vibrating bands across her face. "Also good for facial massage!" whooped Mama Italy, as her young charge's nose and lips slowly changed places.

Looking increasingly wan, the poor girl submitted her thighs to a thorough flogging from the bamboo stick. "Makes slim above the knees!" declared her tormentor ferociously. "And good for any age!" She brought her chiaroscuro face menacingly close to the camera. "Thanks to Vibromass," she whispered hoarsely, "I look at men with new eyes!"

That experience cured me of any misbegotten purchasing urges on the home-exercise front. But still, oh my brothers and sisters, I was weak. I dreamed of changing, of taking my too, too solid flesh and remoulding it – yea, I wished to cast it afresh. I dreamed of making a difference.

Even worse than physical exercise is dieting. I am not too proud to admit it: I have dieted. My diets are never especially ambitious, mind you. They generally take the form of a determination not to eat the little mint they bring around with the bill at my local pizza restaurant. Even then I can only hold firm as long as they keep serving those horrid little blue, sucky mints. When they switch to chewy white Endearmints, all resistance crumbles. Life is a cold, bleak place when you cannot allow yourself an Endearmint.

(Note to editor: was that an endorsement? Do you think the Endearmint people will pay money for that? I am not too proud to admit it: I will accept paid endorsements. Tell them the next book will be called *Who Moved My Endearmints?*)

My diets generally take the form of a determination not to eat the little mint they bring around with the bill at my local pizza restaurant.

Still, things were coming to a sorry pass. I found myself one night, down at the Chalk 'n Cue, hovering on the cusp, the very cusp, of ordering a lite beer, when suddenly clarity came to me. (There is a barmaid down at the Chalk 'n Cue named Clarity, but I am not talking about her. I mean the real clarity, the kind that comes to a man when he has reached his lowest ebb. Of course Clarity also comes to a man when he has reached his lowest ebb – indeed, very often it is the frequency of her return that brings a man to his lowest ebb in the first place – but I am not, as I say, talking about her.)

I thought: What am I doing? Will this lite beer make me happy? This dream of having a six-pack stomach instead of a keg – is this not my desert elephant? I must seize my inner ostrich egg! I must make a virtue of my failing!

Enough is enough, I decided. Enough of the tyranny of the trim. Enough of hiding and skulking and wrapping my midriff in tinfoil. (By the way, when wrapping your midriff in tinfoil, does the shiny side go in or out? No, don't answer that. I don't care any more.) I am a man, damn it, and a protuberant belly is my birthright. My washboard stomach has become something more closely resembling a twin-tub, and I don't care who knows it. Besides, I live a thousand kilometres from the beach and I can always wear loose shirts.

So that is how I reconciled myself to my weaker self, and I have gone further. I am inviting all good men and true to stand beside me. Well, not right beside me. About an arm's length will do. I want you to march with me in the cause of Belly Liberation. Negotiations are under way to stage the nation's first Tummy Pride march early in the new year.

(I won't be there myself, I'm afraid. Because, come to think of it, I am not big on marching. Even the thought of facing the next day after the last day of February tends to make me wheeze and become red in the face. Still, it should be a fun occasion, and I am assured there will be plenty of snacks).

Much time and money and genetic history went into the making of these bellies – let us not disavow them. C'mon, chant it with me now: "We drink beer, we're here, we're everywhere. Get used to us."

Conclusion

The time is drawing near when I must leave you. No, do not weep – it is the way of all things. The rose loses its bloom, beavers chew down trees that dam the mighty river, one day Graeme Hart will no longer present the weather after the 8 o'clock news. To all things there is a season, and already I feel the first stirrings of the gentle autumn breeze. Plus, I didn't get much of an advance for this book, and I have to start doing some other work, before the men from the corner cafe come around to repossess my cigarettes.

Sometimes the universe works in mysterious ways. There is an old man who lives next door to me. He is not the neighbour I borrow ice from and whose Sunday newspaper I sometimes steal – those are the Katzes in number 27. The old man who lives next door to me doesn't take the Sunday paper.

I had never had an extended conversation with the old man. I have always considered him a little creepy, to be honest, because he keeps a collection of life-sized plaster geese standing in the bottom of his garden and occasionally I see him taking them plates of cookies and, on winter nights, a thermos of what I have always assumed is coffee, although it may very well be soup. Sometimes when I have been working too late I sneak over the garden wall and hide his plaster birds under a bush, or arrange them in humorously obscene positions. It gets him no end of riled up. He jumps up and down and yells: "Who has been tampering with my birds?" It's not much, but it amuses me.

Other than that, there had not been much contact between us. Sometimes we would nod to each other over the garden wall, and he would say, "Did you hear those cats fighting in the street last night?"

And I would say, "No."

And he would narrow his eyes and say: "Oh, well, perhaps it was just that music you play till all hours." Then he would stalk inside and close the door. In fact, now that I come to think about it, I have never really liked that old man. But while I was writing this book, a curious thing happened. One afternoon I saw the old man out in the garden, thumbing through a tatty paperback and reading aloud to his geese. I saw the title of the tatty paperback and my blood ran cold. It was *Tuesdays with Morrie.*

I took to staying inside after that, but I couldn't hide forever. The old man next door – let's call him Bill, because that's his name – took to lurking near the garden fence, waiting for me to emerge. One day he caught me as I was carrying out a cardboard box of empty bottles.

"Ahoy, young man," he said, "how would you like to come over for tea?"

"Tea?" I said.

"Oh, all right," he frowned, squinting at the empty bottles. "Bourbon then. Shall we say Tuesday? I think we're Tuesday people, don't you?"

I wasn't planning to visit Bill, but then Tuesday rolled round and I was moping around in my garden, wondering how in the world to write this conclusion. Conclusions, I have always felt, demand solutions, or at least resolutions. But I had no solutions or resolutions, not because I am too lazy too think them up – or at least, not *only* because I am too lazy to think them up – but because solutions and resolutions are what got the world into this mess in the first place. When you put your ear to your inner ostrich egg, that faint and reedy voice you hear echoing back to you, like the waves lapping at the sides of a whiskey tumbler, is saying: "*There are no answers! There are no answers!*"

(When I put my ear to my whiskey tumbler, the waves tend to be saying: "*Drink me! Drink me!*" but I guess that is much the same thing.)

All that moping and thinking about whiskey tumblers began to work on my mind a little, and, before I knew it, I found myself standing on Bill's doorstep. He came to the door wearing baggy clothes and carrying a walking stick that he sometimes forgot to lean on.

"Come in," he said. "Did you bring a tape recorder? No? Never mind, you can take notes."

Bill's plan was clear. Bill was intending to pass his wisdom on to the world. He settled back in his chair and steepled his fingers and looked at the ceiling as though deep in thought.

Then he would say things like: "You know what I have always thought? I have always thought that we should learn to forgive ourselves before we can learn to forgive others." And: "It is my opinion that we should accept the past as past, without denying it or discarding it." And: "Accept what you are able to do and what you are not able to do."

At first I just nodded politely and said "Mmm", and "Very true", and similar things that people say when they don't know what to say, but when he said "Love is the only rational act", I just couldn't bear it any more.

"Bill," I said, "didn't Morrie say all of that?"

So Bill decided to pass on some wisdom of his own. Most of what he had to offer I had heard before, mainly from my own father. My father was a font of good advice. "Never mix your drinks," my dad used to say, "when you can get the barman to mix them for you." Plus: "Do not wear white socks in public, unless you are a tennis player or a newborn babe." And also: "Never trust a short man."

Soon Bill was running short on wisdom, and I was running low on bourbon. I started making motions to leave. "You know," said Bill with a hint of desperation in his voice, "sometimes the universe works in mysterious ways." I pondered that. It is true, in some respects. I still don't know how light can manage to be both particle and wave at the same time, and I have never managed to find out what direction water goes down a plughole if the plughole is directly on the equator. Perhaps Bill would be of some value after all.

"Go on," I said, taking out a pen and pretending to take notes. That stumped him again. The universe does work in mysterious ways, but it is generally easier to say so than to give concrete examples.

"How come your phone can go all day without ringing," he said, "then the moment you make a call, you get two incoming calls at the same time?"

"Hm," I said.

"Uh, and, uh, have you ever wondered what the water level of the ocean would be if sponges didn't grow in it?"

I suddenly took pity on the poor old guy. I rose from my seat and placed my hand on his shoulder, but neither of us liked that, so I took my hand off his shoulder again and sat down hurriedly.

"Bill," I said kindly, "there is no law that says being old means you have to be wise. Wisdom is for people trying to sell books."

He looked at me with mute and grateful eyes. We sat there a while, looking at each other. "The Massagetae, Bill, were a tribe of the Scythian people who occupied the land to the east of the Caspian Sea around 600 BC," I told him. "They venerated old people, Bill. They looked after them, and doffed their caps to them, and they never demanded that the old people contribute anything by way of wise insights or clever maxims. They accepted that old people had done enough just by getting old. Oldness is enough of a good example."

"The Massagetae, eh?" said Bill, nodding thoughtfully. "Maybe I should have been a Massagetae."

"Well, not necessarily, Bill," I had to confess. "They venerated their oldies until a certain point, then they would throw a big birthday feast for the ancient fellow, swing by his house and at a certain stage of the evening – I would imagine sometime after the speeches, and after the first round of drinks – they would kill the birthday boy, boil his flesh and add it to the stew."

"Oh," said Bill.

"Yes," I said, "it wasn't all fun and games and tribal wisdom, living in ancient times."

"Savages," said Bill gloomily.

"You should see the Mayans," I said. And then I said: "Life is simple, Bill. It is enough that you are alive, and you seem more or less continent, and you can watch television whenever you want, and you are not actively participating in the commercial hunting of minke whales. Plus you have your geese, Bill. Don't forget your geese."

He nodded thoughtfully.

"Don't put so much pressure on yourself," I said. "Leave wisdom for the people who feel their lives are empty without it. They are sad people, Bill. They are desperate people. You and me, we can get along just fine without it." But then I remembered that these days people only really listen to aphorisms, so I said: "You know, Bill, when you think about it, wisdom is just another word for living well."

I don't really know what that means, but it seemed to make him happier. We got along just fine after that, and when the bourbon was finished and I weaved my way to the door, it was just like we were old acquaintances. As he waved me goodbye, I turned and looked him in the eye and said: "I'm okay, Bill, and you … you live next door."

It was one of those moments that you never forget, no matter how you try.

But perhaps Bill was sent to help me write this final chapter. (If so, it is a very depressing thought. Imagine living an entire life, complete with its full allotment of heartache, trauma and bad haircuts, simply so that some mouthy fellow next door can finish his book in time to make the Christmas sales list.) After I arrived home, once I had buried my keys under a loose tile in the kitchen, I fell to musing. You and I have come a long way together – well, longish – and I am afraid I may have been doing us a disservice. I know I have been referring to us as "lazy" all through this book, but maybe "lazy" isn't the right word. We may not want to go to unnecessary exertion, but the important word there is "unnecessary", not "exertion".

This world is awash with guff, with humbug and bushwah and just plain dumbness, and it is a full-time job to wade through it all without becoming so tired that you just lie down and let it roll over you and become one with the dumbness. Stupidity clothes itself in many outfits – the postal services, Spice Girls pursuing solo careers, that little bastard Jamie Oliver – and one of its current looks for this and the next few seasons is to dress up like wisdom.

It is a full-time job to wade through it all without becoming so tired that you just lie down and let it roll over you and become one with the dumbness.

Our job – yours and mine – is to shrug off the stupidity,

to push it behind us, and above all to enrich ourselves while we're about it. I've held up my end of the bargain by writing this book, and hopefully by selling it too. How you do your job is up to you. I have no ideas off the top of my head, but do let me know if there is anything of a practical nature I can do to help.

I was going to wrap up with an explanation of the title, but I don't think I'll bother now. There was never really any cheese, was there? And even if there had been, I would probably have eaten it, rather than moved it around. The cheese was just a cunning device to get you to read to the end. And here you are, so I suppose it must have worked.

EPILOGUE

Bill and I are good neighbours now. There is warmth in our good-morning nods. But of course, old habits die hard. When I work too late I still get the urge to shinny over the wall and tiptoe across his lawn and rearrange his plaster aviary. Just this morning I woke to the sound of Bill shouting and cursing and rooting around in the shrubbery for one of his birds.

I opened the bedroom window and I leant outside. I yelled across the wall. "Relax, Bill!" I yelled. "Relax!"

Bill looked across to me, and our eyes met once more. "Don't worry, Bill," I said. "It was me, Bill. I moved your geese."

You will notice that the final pages of this book are blank. There is no writing on them. They are – unless the staff members at your local bookstore have been playing silly buggers with their felt-tipped pens – entirely free of doodles, graffiti, bar-graphs, shopping lists and marginalia. Do not consider yourself cheated. Think of these pages not as a disappointment but as an opportunity.

Blank pages in a book are the literary equivalent of unscheduled free minutes in your day. It is obviously my duty to suggest you put these pages to some improving end – jotting down preliminary thoughts for your impending assault on Fermat's last theorem, for instance, or making notes for the planned epic sonnet cycle that will revolutionise the way we read poetry for evermore – but in truth there are altogether simpler and more rewarding uses to which these pages may be put. For instance:

- You may be reading this book in warm weather, perhaps wearing woollen garments you donned this morning in the mistaken belief that the afternoon would turn chilly. If so, these pages are eminently suitable for blotting perspiration from your upper lip. Do not hesitate to do this: a moist upper lip causes you to resemble Richard Nixon. It is unattractive. You are unlikely to get lucky with a moist upper lip. Plus, I wouldn't want any passers-by to think that this is the sort of book read by people with moist upper lips.
- Detached from the binding, these pages would be suitable for use in origami, as coasters for your bourbon, or as a do-it-yourself confetti kit.
- You may want to use these pages to make yourself a checklist of everything you have learnt in the preceding pages. Each morning you can rise and greet the world and run through the valuable tips you have gleaned. I shan't dictate what valuable tips you should have gleaned, but if I might make a few suggestions:

- ✓ When life gives you a mango, use it to make sangria.
- ✓ Stupid is as stupid does, so stop doing stupid things.
- ✓ Life is like a box of chocolates – it is overpriced, will make you sick if you have it too quickly, and if other people see you with it, they will try to take bits of it away from you.
- ✓ Think before you speak. Read before you think. Wash your hands before you read.
- ✓ A stitch in time saves seven-and-a-half, eight tops.
- ✓ I'm okay.
- ✓ Do not waste time wondering if the glass is half-empty or half-full. If the glass looks half-anything, it is time to order another round.
- ✓ In life, as in dinner-table conversation, only a cad says everything he means, and only a bore means everything he says.
- ✓ Do not just say no. Do not just do it. These things require circumspection. Just say: "That's for me to know and you to find out." Just say: "Maybe, maybe not." Just say nothing at all.
- ✓ Always leave the party five minutes before you have run out of things to say.

I wish you well, my friends. If you feel your strength failing, flip through this book and soon you will be reminded: "Anything can be faked."